LE CORDON BLEU

HOME COLLECTION

·COOKIES·

PERIPLUS
EDITIONS

contents

recipe ratings ✦ *easy* ✦✦ *a little more care needed* ✦✦✦ *more care needed*

Melting moments

*As their name suggests, these melt-in-the-mouth cookies with their
soft buttercream and jam filling are simply irresistible.*

Preparation time **45 minutes**
Total cooking time **20 minutes per baking sheet**
Makes about 30

1 cup unsalted butter, at room temperature
3/4 confectioners' sugar, sifted
1 teaspoon finely grated lemon rind
2 egg yolks
2 1/3 cups all-purpose flour
2 1/2 tablespoons raspberry jam, beaten
confectioners' sugar, to dust

BUTTERCREAM
1/3 cup sugar
1 egg white
1/3 cup unsalted butter, at room temperature

1 Preheat the oven to 350°F. Brush two baking sheets with melted butter. Using a wooden spoon or an electric mixer, cream together the butter, confectioners' sugar and lemon rind until light and fluffy.

2 Add the egg yolks and mix thoroughly. Sift in the flour and stir with a wooden spoon until the mixture

comes together to make a smooth soft paste. Spoon into a pastry bag with a 1/3-inch star nozzle.

3 Pipe enough 5/8–3/4-inch rosettes to fill the prepared baking sheets, spacing well apart (see Chef's techniques, page 63). Bake for 10–12 minutes, or until the edges are golden. Cool on a wire rack. Repeat with the remaining mixture, preparing the baking sheets as in step 1.

4 To make the buttercream, in a small saucepan, over low heat, dissolve 1/4 cup of the sugar in 1 tablespoon water, stirring occasionally. Increase the heat and bring to a boil. Simmer, without stirring, for 3–5 minutes. To prevent crystals of sugar forming, wipe down the sides of the pan with a brush dipped in water. Meanwhile, beat the egg white until stiff. Add the remaining sugar and beat until stiff and shiny and peaks form when the beaters are lifted. While beating the mixture, pour in the bubbling syrup in a thin steady stream, aiming between the bowl and the beaters. Continue to beat until the mixture is cold. Gradually add the soft butter.

5 Divide the cookies into pairs and spread jam on the flat side of one of each pair. Using a plain 1/4-inch nozzle, pipe a little buttercream onto the other cookie, sandwich the two together and dust lightly with sifted confectioners' sugar.

Florentines

Attributed to Austrian bakers, this wonderful mixture of sugar, butter, cream, nuts and fruit has its origins in Italy. Crisp to eat, they have the added allure of a chocolate base, which is optional though traditional.

*Preparation time **20 minutes + 10 minutes standing***
*Total cooking time **15 minutes per baking sheet***
Makes 25–30

1/2 cup unsalted butter

1/2 cup sugar

**1/2 cup candied orange or mixed citrus peel,
 finely chopped**

**2 tablespoons glacé (candied) cherries,
 cut into 8 pieces**

2/3 cup blanched sliced almonds

3/4 cup blanched almonds, chopped

2 tablespoons heavy cream

8 oz. good-quality semisweet chocolate, chopped

1 Preheat the oven to 350°F. Brush two baking sheets with melted butter.

2 Melt the butter in a small saucepan, stir in the sugar, slowly bring to a boil and remove from the heat. Add the candied peel, cherries, the sliced and chopped almonds and mix well. Beat the cream until it is thick and gently stir it into the warm mixture. Set aside for about 10 minutes, or until cool and thick.

3 Using a heaped teaspoon of mixture for each Florentine, spoon on enough mounds of the mixture to fill the two baking sheets (see Chef's techniques, page 63). Space well apart as the cookies will spread. Bake for about 5 minutes, or until lightly set. Using a large cutter or a cup, shape the spread mixture into neat rounds by pulling in the edges. Return to the oven for 4 minutes. Reshape with the cutter and let cool for 3 minutes, or until firm enough to remove from the baking sheet. Carefully lift them with a palette knife and cool on a wire rack. Repeat with the remaining mixture, preparing the baking sheets as instructed in step 1. Warm the mixture a little if it has cooled too much to spoon easily.

4 Place the chocolate in the top of a double boiler over steaming water, off the stove. Make sure the bottom of the insert does not touch the water. Stir occasionally until the chocolate has melted and let cool to room temperature. Using a palette knife, spread onto the smooth underside of the Florentines. Return them to the rack until the chocolate is just setting. Run a fork through the chocolate to make wavy lines and let set at room temperature.

Chef's tip Florentines make excellent petits fours if made with 1/2 teaspoon of mixture. They will store in an airtight container for up to 1 week.

English rout biscuits

These decorative pressed cookies are excellent served with tea, coffee or even a glass of wine.

Preparation time **15 minutes + drying overnight**
Total cooking time **10 minutes**
Makes about 24

1/3 **cup fine semolina or rice flour**
2/3 **cup ground almonds**
I cup confectioners' sugar
1/4 **teaspoon ground cinnamon**
I egg white
halved glacé (candied) cherries or halved almonds,
   to decorate
3 tablespoons strained apricot jam

1   Sprinkle two baking sheets with the semolina or rice flour. Sift the almonds, sugar and cinnamon into a bowl. Add the egg white and mix to a very stiff paste.

2   Spoon the mixture into a pastry bag. Using a large star nozzle, pipe the mixture onto the prepared baking sheets in rosettes 11/4 inches wide (see Chef's techniques, page 63) or *fleurs-de-lys* 11/4 inches long. Place half a glacé cherry or half an almond in the center of each cookie. Leave uncovered overnight to dry.

3   Preheat the oven to 475°F. Bake for 8–10 minutes, or until the cookies are just browned on the edges.

4   Place the jam in a small saucepan with 1 tablespoon water until melted. Strain and brush over the cookies.

Chef's tips The mixture should be very stiff and even difficult to pipe to obtain a crisp, dry result.

   A *fleur-de-lys* is a heraldic symbol, and the shape represents a lily, with its three distinct petals.

Sugar cookies

Whether flavored with almond, vanilla, cinnamon or lemon, these sugar-coated cookies are always popular. This practical recipe allows you to freeze leftover dough, thus enabling you to produce freshly made cookies within minutes for unexpected visitors.

Preparation time **15 minutes + 25 minutes refrigeration**
Total cooking time **15 minutes per baking sheet**
Makes 45

1²/3 cups all-purpose flour
pinch of salt
2 teaspoons baking powder
¹/2 cup unsalted butter, at room temperature
I cup sugar
I egg, lightly beaten
¹/4 teaspoon almond extract
¹/4 cup Demerara sugar

1 Sift together the flour, salt and baking powder. In a bowl, beat the butter with a wooden spoon or electric mixer until smooth. Add the sugar gradually to the butter, beating constantly until pale and creamy. Pour in the egg, a little at a time, beating well after each addition. Stir in the almond extract.

2 Add the flour to the butter mixture and mix well. Cover the dough with plastic wrap and place in the refrigerator to chill for about 15 minutes, or until firm.

3 Once the mixture is firm, shape it into a long roll about 2 inches in diameter. Roll the dough in plastic wrap, twisting the ends to seal well. Return the dough to the refrigerator for another 10 minutes. Unwrap and roll the dough in the Demerara sugar until the outside is well coated, but the ends are clean. Refrigerate the dough until needed.

4 Preheat the oven to 350°F. Brush two baking sheets with melted butter. Slice enough of the chilled roll into rounds 1/4 inch thick to fill the baking sheets. Place on the prepared baking sheets, 11/2 inches apart. Refrigerate the rest of the mixture. Bake for about 12–15 minutes, or until golden, then transfer to a wire rack to cool. Repeat with the remaining mixture, preparing the baking sheets with melted butter as instructed above.

Chef's tips As an alternative to almond extract, flavor the dough with vanilla extract, cinnamon or finely grated lemon rind. You could also roll the dough in colored sugar crystals intead of the Demerara sugar.

This dough freezes wonderfully for up to 4 weeks. Place in the freezer when the dough is shaped in a long roll. When you want to use it, simply slice the frozen dough into rounds using a serrated bread knife. The cookies can be baked frozen, but they may need a few minutes longer in the oven.

Orange tuiles

The delicious orange, almond and Grand Marnier flavor of these delicate crisp tuiles *make them a perfect accompaniment to vanilla ice cream or a fresh fruit sorbet.*

Preparation time **15 minutes**
Total cooking time **5 minutes per baking sheet**
Makes 60

¹/4 cup orange juice
finely grated rind of 1 orange
3 tablespoons Grand Marnier
1 cup sugar
¹/3 cup unsalted butter, melted but cooled
1¹/4 cups almonds, finely chopped
1 cup all-purpose flour

1 Preheat the oven to 375°F. Brush two baking sheets with melted butter and refrigerate.
2 Place the orange juice and rind, Grand Marnier and sugar in a bowl. Stir in the melted butter, chopped almonds and flour.
3 Prepare the *tuiles* following the method in the Chef's techniques on page 63. Bake one sheet of *tuiles* at a time for 5 minutes, or until light golden all over. (For removing the *tuiles* from the baking sheet see page 63.) Repeat with the remaining mixture, preparing the baking sheets as instructed in step 1.

Chef's tip The *tuiles* can be stored in an airtight container for up to a week.

Coconut tuiles

Tuile is the French word for tile. These wafers are shaped to represent the slightly rounded, overlapping tiles found on many European roofs, especially around the Mediterranean.

Preparation time **15 minutes**
Total cooking time **5 minutes per baking sheet**
Makes 40

3 small egg whites
1 cup finely shredded or flaked coconut (see Chef's tips)
¹/3 cup sugar
3 tablespoons all-purpose flour
¹/4 cup unsalted butter, melted, but cooled

1 Preheat the oven to 375°F. Brush two baking sheets with melted butter and refrigerate.
2 Lightly beat the egg whites with a fork to loosen them. Add the coconut, sugar, flour and butter and stir together.
3 Prepare the *tuiles* following the method in the Chef's techniques on page 63. Bake one sheet of *tuiles* at a time for 5 minutes, or until light golden all over. (For removing the *tuiles* from the baking sheet see page 63.) Repeat with the remaining mixture, preparing the baking sheets as instructed in step 1.

Chef's tips If using sweetened coconut, reduce the sugar slightly.

To make almond *tuiles*, use ¹/2 cup finely chopped almonds in place of the coconut.

The *tuiles* can be stored in an airtight container for up to a week.

Orange tuiles (top) and Coconut tuiles

Sablés nantais

*Generally round with fluted edges, these golden crumbly cookies melt in the mouth. It is due
to this delicate crumbly texture that these cookies from the French region of Nantes are called* sablés,
from the French word sable, *meaning sand.*

*Preparation time **15 minutes + 1 hour 20 minutes
refrigeration***
*Total cooking time **12 minutes per baking sheet***
Makes about 50

❁

3/4 cup unsalted butter, at room temperature
2²/3 cups confectioners' sugar
I egg, lightly beaten
4 egg yolks
2 teaspoons vanilla extract
3¹/3 cups all-purpose flour
pinch of salt
¹/2 teaspoon baking powder
pinch of ground cinnamon
two drops strong coffee or coffee extract

1 Preheat the oven to 375°F. Brush two baking sheets
with melted butter and refrigerate.
2 Using a wooden spoon or electric mixer, cream
together the butter and the sugar. Mix together half of
the beaten egg with the egg yolks and reserve the
remaining half egg. Gradually add the egg yolk mixture
to the butter mixture, beating well after each addition.
Stir in the vanilla.

3 Sift the flour, salt, baking powder and cinnamon
together and fold into the butter mixture. Using a
plastic spatula, scrape the mixture onto a large piece of
plastic wrap, pat lightly to flatten. Wrap and refrigerate
for at least 1 hour.
4 In a small bowl, lightly beat the remaining 1/2 egg
with the coffee extract and set aside.
5 Roll out the pastry to a 1/8–1/4 inch thickness
between two sheets of waxed paper (see Chef's
techniques, page 63). Cut out enough shapes using a
2-inch round fluted cutter to fill the two baking sheets,
then return the remaining mixture to the refrigerator.
Place the shapes on the baking sheets and chill in the
refrigerator for about 20 minutes. Brush with the egg
and coffee mixture. Using a fork, make crisscross
patterns on top of the cookies. Bake for about
12 minutes, or until golden. Remove from the baking
sheets and cool on a wire rack. Repeat with the
remaining mixture, preparing the baking sheets as
instructed in step 1.

Chef's tip The buttery pastry will soften quickly in a
warm kitchen. Roll out in batches to keep the pastry
cool and easy to work with. *Sablés nantais* will keep,
stored in an airtight container, for up to 1 week.

Rum and raisin cookies

The classic combination of rum and raisins gives excellent results in these thin crisp cookies.
Delicious with a cup of tea or coffee, or served with vanilla ice cream.

*Preparation time **15 minutes + 1 hour soaking***
*Total cooking time **7 minutes per baking sheet***
Makes about 25

1/4 cup raisins, finely chopped (see Chef's tip)
3 tablespoons rum
3 tablespoons unsalted butter,
  at room temperature
1/3 cup confectioners' sugar
2–3 drops vanilla extract
I egg, lightly beaten
1/2 cup all-purpose flour

1 Place the raisins in a small bowl, pour in the rum, cover with plastic wrap. Let soak for at least 1 hour. Preheat the oven to 375°F. Brush two baking sheets with softened butter, then refrigerate until set. Brush the sheets with some more butter to make a double coating and refrigerate again.

2 In a large bowl, soften the butter using a wooden spoon or an electric mixer. Gradually beat in the confectioners' sugar, then continue to beat until the mixture is light and fluffy. Add the vanilla. Gradually add the egg to the butter mixture, beating well after each addition to prevent curdling or separation.

3 Sift the flour and add it to the butter mixture, beating well until smooth. Stir in the soaked, chopped raisins and rum and mix well.

4 Spoon the mixture into a pastry bag fitted with a 1/2-inch plain nozzle. Pipe enough 1-inch wide rounds to fill the two prepared baking sheets, spacing them at least 11/4 inches apart as they will spread during baking.

5 To encourage the cookies to spread, bang the baking sheets heavily once on the work surface. Bake for 6–7 minutes, or until golden brown at the edges, but slightly paler in the center. Remove from the baking sheets and transfer to a wire rack to cool. Repeat with the remaining mixture, preparing the baking sheets as instructed in step 1.

Chef's tips If you find the raisins stick to the knife when chopping, add a little flour from the recipe as you chop.

As a variation, you can add a tablespoon of chopped candied angelica and glacé (candied) cherries for a jewel-like cookie.

Eponges

The name éponge, meaning sponge in French, was probably given to these almond-flavored cookies because of their resemblance to sea sponges. The crunchy almond coating provides a good contrast to the light meringue texture of these petits fours.

*Preparation time **20 minutes***
*Total cooking time **10 minutes***
Makes about 20

2 egg whites
2 tablespoons sugar
1/3 cup confectioners' sugar
1/3 cup blanched almonds, ground
1 cup blanched almonds, finely chopped
1/4 cup seedless raspberry jam
confectioners' sugar, to dust

1 Preheat the oven to 375°F. Brush two baking sheets with melted butter, sprinkle with flour and tap off the excess.

2 Beat the egg whites and a pinch of the sugar with a balloon whisk or electric mixer for 2 minutes, or until soft peaks form. Slowly add the remaining sugar, beating well after each addition. Sift the confectioners' sugar and ground almonds together and fold in until well mixed. Spoon the mixture into a pastry bag fitted with a 1/2-inch plain round nozzle. Pipe small, evenly spaced 11/4-inch wide, domed rounds onto the prepared baking sheets. Sprinkle with the chopped almonds and bake for 7–10 minutes, or until golden. Remove from the baking sheets and cool on a wire rack.

3 When cool, arrange the *éponges*, flat-side-up, in pairs. Spread a little jam on one of the pair and sandwich with the other. Dust with sifted confectioners' sugar.

Chef's tip If you are baking more than one sheet of cookies in a non-convection oven, swap them around halfway through baking to make sure they cook evenly.

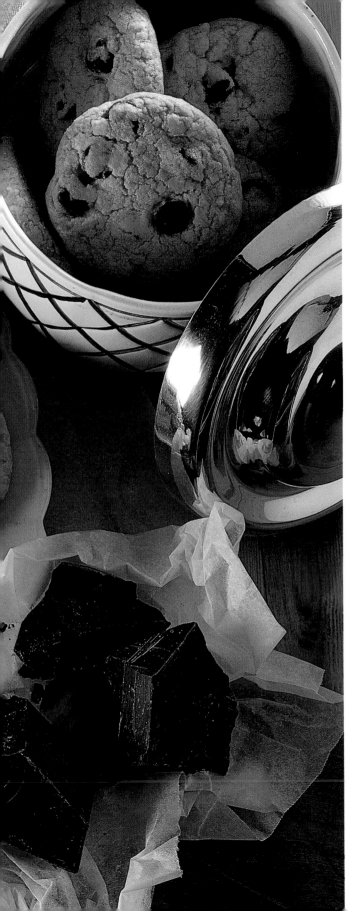

Chocolate chip cookies

These cookies, originally created at the Toll House Inn in Massachusetts in the 1920's, became so popular that small round chocolate pieces, known as "chips," were marketed especially for them.

Preparation time **20 minutes**
Total cooking time **20 minutes per baking sheet**
Makes 24

¹/2 **cup unsalted butter, at room temperature**
¹/2 **cup soft brown sugar**
¹/3 **cup sugar**
I egg, lightly beaten
¹/4 **teaspoon vanilla extract**
I ¹/4 **cups all-purpose flour**
pinch of baking powder
¹/2 **cup ground almonds**
I cup semisweet chocolate chips

1 Preheat the oven to 350°F. Brush two baking sheets with melted butter and refrigerate until set.
2 Using a wooden spoon or an electric mixer, cream the butter and sugars until light and fluffy. Gradually add the egg and vanilla, beating well after each addition.
3 Sift the flour, baking powder and ground almonds together. Fold half into the creamed mixture. When almost incorporated, add the rest of the sifted mixture, then add the chocolate chips as you fold.
4 Divide into 24 portions and roll into balls. Place the balls, spaced well apart, on the two prepared baking sheets and flatten slightly. Bake for 15–20 minutes, or until golden brown. Remove from the baking sheets while still hot and transfer to a cooling rack. Repeat with the remaining mixture, preparing the baking sheets as instructed in step 1. Store in an airtight container.

Macaroons

These vanilla-flavored macaroons, crisp on the outside with surprisingly soft, moist centers, can be sandwiched together with different flavored fillings, such as fruit jams or melted chocolate.

Preparation time **15 minutes**
Total cooking time **20 minutes per baking sheet**
Makes 40

2/3 cup ground almonds
2 cups confectioners' sugar
4 egg whites
2–3 drops vanilla extract
pinch of sugar
4 oz. semisweet chocolate, chopped

1 Place two baking sheets together and line the top sheet with waxed paper (this double thickness sheet will prevent the bottom of the macaroons from over-browning during cooking). Preheat the oven to 325°F.
2 Sift the almonds and confectioners' sugar into a bowl, then sift again to make sure they are thoroughly mixed. In a separate bowl, beat the egg whites and vanilla with a pinch of sugar until stiff and shiny and the mixture forms peaks when the beaters are lifted.

3 Using a plastic spatula, gently fold the dry ingredients into the egg white, trying not to lose any air. The mixture should be shiny and soft, not liquid.
4 Spoon the mixture into a pastry bag fitted with a 1/4-inch nozzle. Pipe enough 1 1/4-inch wide rounds to fill the prepared baking sheet, leaving a little space between them. Bake for about 15–20 minutes, or until golden and crisp, checking the macaroons frequently during baking. Cool on the baking sheet for a few minutes, then remove to a wire rack. Repeat with the remaining mixture, preparing the baking sheets as instructed in step 1.
5 Place the chocolate in the top of a double boiler over steaming water, off the stove. Make sure the bottom of the insert doesn't touch the water. Stir until the chocolate melts. Sandwich the macaroons together in pairs with the chocolate and let cool.

Chef's tip If you are baking more than one sheet of cookies in a non-convection oven, swap them around halfway through baking to make sure they cook evenly.

Lunettes

*Lunettes is the French word for spectacles. Shaped to represent spectacles,
these cookies are elegant with tea and coffee, but also fun for children.*

*Preparation time **30 minutes + 30 minutes refrigeration***
*Total cooking time **10 minutes per baking sheet***
*Makes **10***

1/4 cup ground almonds
1 cup all-purpose flour
3 tablespoons unsalted butter
1 teaspoon finely grated lemon rind
3 tablespoons sugar
1/2 egg, beaten
1/4 cup strained apricot jam
confectioners' sugar, to dust
1/4 cup raspberry jam

1 Preheat the oven to 350°F. Brush two baking sheets with melted butter and dust lightly with flour. Sift together the almonds and flour.

2 Using a wooden spoon or electric mixer, cream together the butter, lemon rind and sugar until light and fluffy. Add the egg, a little at a time, beating well after each addition. Add the flour and almonds and stir together to form a rough dough. Pull the dough together by hand to form a ball, wrap in plastic wrap, flatten slightly and refrigerate for about 30 minutes. Roll out the dough between two sheets of waxed paper to a 1/8 inch thickness (see Chef's techniques, page 63).

3 Using a 3-inch oval cutter, cut out about 20 cookies and transfer as many as will fit comfortably to the prepared baking sheets. Using a 1/2–5/8-inch round cutter, or the end of a 1/2-inch piping nozzle, cut out two holes from half of the oval cookies. These will become the tops of the *lunettes*. Refrigerate the rest of the dough until needed.

4 Bake for 10 minutes, or until light golden. While still warm, remove the cookies from the baking sheets to a wire rack. Repeat with the remaining dough, preparing the sheets as instructed in step 1.

5 Warm the apricot jam, brush over the base of the whole cookies and sandwich together with a cookie with holes in the top.

6 Dust with confectioners' sugar. Beat the raspberry jam in a bowl until it flows. Fill a pastry bag fitted with a 1/4-inch plain nozzle and fill in each of the holes on the sandwiched cookies with the jam. If you don't have a pastry bag, drop the jam from the tip of a teaspoon.

Shortbread

Shortbread can be made with all-purpose flour alone, however the texture is greatly enhanced by using a combination of flours. Adding rice flour produces a light result, while semolina will give a crunchy texture.

*Preparation time **10 minutes + 10 minutes refrigeration***
*Total cooking time **25 minutes***
Makes 8

1/2 cup unsalted butter, at room temperature
1/4 cup sugar
I cup all-purpose flour
1/3 cup rice flour or fine semolina, sifted twice
2 tablespoons sugar, to dust

1 Preheat the oven to 350°F. Beat the butter in a wide bowl until smooth. Gradually beat in the sugar. Add the all-purpose flour and rice flour or semolina and stir with a fork until well blended.

2 Press the mixture into a 7–8-inch springform or round cake pan with a removable base. Make sure that the mixture is level and pierce the surface evenly with a fork. Place in the refrigerator to chill for 10 minutes.

3 Sprinkle the surface of the shortbread with the extra sugar and bake for 25 minutes, or until golden.

4 While the shortbread is still hot, carefully remove from the pan and cut into eight wedges, using a large sharp knife. Don't separate the pieces of shortbread or they will dry out. After 5 minutes, the shortbread will be firmer—transfer to a wire rack and sprinkle with a little more sugar.

Chef's tips The shortbread may rise or wrinkle slightly during baking—this is quite normal.

The shortbread will keep for up to a week if stored in an airtight container or wrapped in foil.

Langues-de-chat

Langue-de-chat, the French term for cat's tongue, is the name given to these wafer cookies due to their resemblance to the shape of a cat's tongue. Delicately flavored, light and crisp, they may be served with a sweet soufflé or as an elegant accompaniment to coffee.

*Preparation time **15 minutes***
*Total cooking time **10 minutes per baking sheet***
Makes about 50

3/4 cup confectioners' sugar
1/3 cup unsalted butter, at room temperature
3–4 drops vanilla extract
3 egg whites, lightly beaten
3/4 cup all-purpose flour

1 Preheat the oven to 400°F. Brush two baking sheets with melted butter and refrigerate.
2 Using a wooden spoon or electric mixer, cream the sugar and butter together. When the mixture is pale and light, beat in the vanilla.
3 Add the egg whites slowly, beating constantly and being careful not to allow the mixture to curdle. If it does, add a large pinch of the measured flour.

4 Sift the flour into the bowl, then using a large metal spoon or plastic spatula, gently fold the flour into the butter mixture, mixing lightly until combined. Spoon into a pastry bag fitted with a 1/3-inch plain nozzle and pipe enough 3-inch lengths to fill the prepared baking sheets. Leave at least 2 inches between the cookies as they will spread during baking. Bake for 7–10 minutes, until the edges are golden brown but the centers yellow.
5 Use a palette knife to remove the cookies from the baking sheet while they are still warm. If they cool and become too brittle to move, return them to the oven to warm for a moment or two. Repeat with the remaining mixture, preparing the sheets as instructed in step 1.

Chef's tip *Langues-de-chat* may be used to line molds that are then filled with light creamy mixtures such as mousses, chilled until set and turned out. Or they can be placed around the sides of cream-coated cakes. Store in an airtight container for up to 2 weeks.

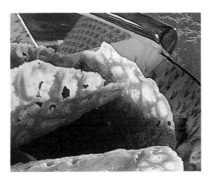

Ginger thins

*Crisp, thin and lacy, these ginger-flavored wafers are delicious
served with ice cream or light, creamy desserts.*

Preparation time 10 minutes
Total cooking time 10 minutes per baking sheet
Makes 12

I tablespoons unsalted butter
2 tablespoons confectioners' sugar
2 tablespoons dark corn syrup
3 tablespoons all-purpose flour
1/2 teaspoon ground ginger
pinch of salt

1 Brush two baking sheets with melted butter and refrigerate until set. Brush once more with butter and refrigerate again. Preheat the oven to 400°F. Cut a round 2 inches in diameter from the center of a piece of plastic (a margarine container lid is perfect for this). This will give you a plastic stencil with a 2-inch round hole in the center.

2 In a saucepan, gently heat the butter, confectioners' sugar and corn syrup, stirring until the sugar has dissolved. Remove from the heat and allow to cool slightly. Sift the flour, ginger and salt together twice and stir into the butter mixture.

3 Prepare the cookies with the plastic stencil, following the method in the Chef's techniques on page 62.

4 Bake for 6–7 minutes, or until golden brown. Immediately lift the wafers from the baking sheet and, while still warm and pliable, shape over a rolling pin or roll them carefully around the rounded handle of a wooden spoon. Leave the shapes to cool on a wire rack. Repeat with the remaining mixture, preparing the baking sheets as instructed in step 1. Warm the mixture a little if it has cooled too much to spoon easily. When cool, immediately place in an airtight container to prevent the wafers going soggy.

Chef's tips If the cookies set on the baking sheet before you can lift them all off, return the baking sheet to the oven to warm them through again.

Try cutting fancy shapes, such as a star or moon, from the plastic for the stencil.

To make cinnamon thins, replace the ground ginger with ground cinnamon.

Amaretti

For a traditional Italian gift, wrap pairs of cookies in colored tissue paper, twisting the ends.

Preparation time **10 minutes**
Total cooking time **15 minutes per baking sheet**
Makes about 40

¹/₂ cup blanched almonds, halved or chopped
¹/₃ cup sugar
1 egg white
1 tablespoon Amaretto liqueur
2 drops almond extract
confectioners' sugar, to dust

1 Preheat the oven to 350°F. Line two baking sheets with waxed paper.
2 Place the almonds and the sugar in a food processor and process to a fine powder. Add the egg white, Amaretto and almond extract and process to make a soft dough.
3 Spoon the mixture into a pastry bag, fitted with a ⁵/₈-inch plain nozzle. Pipe enough 1-inch rounds to fill the two prepared baking sheets, spacing the cookies well apart. Hold the nozzle ¹/₂ inch away from the sheet to make well-rounded shapes. Bake for 12–15 minutes, or until golden. Cool on a wire rack. Repeat with the remaining mixture, preparing the baking sheets as instructed in step 1. Dust with sifted confectioners' sugar while still warm.

Chef's tips For a good result, make sure the almonds and sugar are very finely ground before adding the egg white.

For a variation, top each cookie with half an almond before baking.

Vanilla cookies

These cookies are traditionally served with a glass of sweet wine or Madeira. Enjoy them with tea or coffee or try them with mulled wine when the weather is cold. They are particularly good eaten with poached fruits served in their syrup.

*Preparation time **20 minutes + 5 hours standing time***
*Total cooking time **20 minutes***
Makes 40

1/4 cup sugar
1 egg
1 egg yolk
2–3 drops vanilla extract
1 teaspoon finely grated lemon rind
1/2 cup all-purpose flour
extra sugar, to dust

1 Line two baking sheets with waxed paper.
2 Bring water to a boil in the bottom of a double boiler and remove from the heat. Put the sugar, egg, egg yolk, vanilla and lemon rind in the top of the double boiler and place it over the water, making sure the bottom of the insert does not touch the water. Beat with an electric mixer for 5–10 minutes, or until the mixture becomes thick and mousse-like and leaves a trail as it falls from the beaters. Remove the insert from the water and continue to beat for 5 minutes, or until the mixture is cold.

3 Sift the flour and fold it into the egg mixture. Use a metal spoon or plastic spatula and fold until the flour is only just combined. Spoon the mixture into a pastry bag fitted with a 3/4-inch plain nozzle and pipe rounded mounds of the mixture about 1 inch in diameter and spaced well apart onto the baking sheets. Sprinkle with the extra sugar. Leave the mixture to dry on the baking sheets for 4–5 hours at room temperature. Preheat the oven to 300°F.

4 Bake for 20 minutes, or until golden brown and firm to the touch. Transfer the cookies to a wire rack to cool.

Chef's tip For a variation, you could sandwich two cookies together with a little jam.

Lebkuchen

A traditional Austrian and German spicy soft cookie that comes into its own in winter and especially for Christmas. Delicious served with tea, coffee or mulled wine in wintertime.

Preparation time **30 minutes**
Total cooking time **25 minutes**
Makes 24

1/4 cup chopped mixed candied citrus peel
1 1/4 cups all-purpose flour
large pinch of ground cloves
1/2 teaspoon ground cinnamon
1/2 teaspoon ground ginger
large pinch of ground nutmeg
1/4 teaspoon baking powder
1/2 cup ground almonds
1 egg
1/4 cup dark brown sugar
3/4 cup honey
1/4 cup milk
1 cup confectioners' sugar
1 teaspoon brandy

1 Preheat the oven to 400°F. Brush an 11 x 7 x 2-inch pan with melted butter, line the base with waxed paper and brush with butter. Dust the pan with flour, turning to coat the base and sides thoroughly.

2 Lightly dust a work surface with flour, place the candied peel on it, toss lightly in the flour and then chop finely using a large sharp knife. The flour will stop the peel from sticking to the knife. Sift the flour, cloves, cinnamon, ginger, nutmeg and baking powder into a large bowl. Add the chopped peel and stir in the almonds.

3 Place the egg and brown sugar in a bowl and beat with an electric mixer until increased in volume and pale in color. Beat in the honey, then the milk. Pour into the flour mixture and stir briskly until the mixture resembles a batter.

4 Pour the mixture into the pan and spread evenly to the corners. Bake on the middle shelf of the oven for about 20–25 minutes, or until just springy to the light touch of a finger. While the Lebkuchen is cooking, prepare the frosting.

5 To make the frosting, sift the confectioners' sugar into a small bowl, add 1 tablespoon water and the brandy and mix with a wooden spoon to a thick coating consistency. It should run, but leave a trail as it falls back. If it doesn't fall from the spoon, it may need a little more water.

6 Loosen the sides of the Lebkuchen and turn it out of the pan onto a baking sheet, then invert onto a wire rack, crust-side-up. Brush the top with the frosting while it is still warm—it will run to give a thin glaze. Leave to cool and then cut into 8 slices lengthwise and 3 across to make 24 pieces. Remove from the paper. Store in an airtight container for up to 1 month.

Chef's tips Lebkuchen may be served without frosting. You can also cool them and then put on the frosting very thinly, coloring small amounts differently to give pink, white and yellow cookies from the same batch. Or, perhaps dip the top of some into melted semisweet chocolate. A small sprinkling of tiny multicolored candy sprinkles or nonpareils is also traditional.

Thumbprint cookies

The name given to these simple but delicious cookies comes from the method—after placing small balls of dough onto a baking sheet, indentations are made with the thumb and then filled with jam.

Preparation time **35 minutes + 30 minutes refrigeration**
Total cooking time: **25 minutes per baking sheet**
Makes about 36

2 cups all-purpose flour
1/4 teaspoon baking soda
1/4 teaspoon salt
I cup unsalted butter, at room temperature
2/3 cup confectioners' sugar
I egg
I teaspoon vanilla extract
I 1/4 cups walnuts or almonds, chopped
raspberry jam

1 Preheat the oven to 350°F. Brush two baking sheets with melted butter.
2 Sift together the flour, baking soda and salt. Cream together the butter and confectioners' sugar until smooth and creamy. Add the egg and vanilla and beat well. Mix in the dry ingredients until completely blended. Cover and refrigerate for 30 minutes.

3 Scoop up heaped teaspoons of the dough and roll into balls about 1 inch in diameter. Roll the balls in the chopped nuts, pressing the nuts in well. Use enough pieces to fill the prepared baking sheets, spacing them about 2 inches apart. Press the center of each ball with your thumb to make a deep impression. Using the handle of a spoon or a pastry bag fitted with a small plain nozzle, fill the impressions with the jam, being careful not to overfill.
4 Bake for 20–25 minutes, or until the nuts are toasted. Remove the cookies from the baking sheets and cool on a wire rack. Repeat with the remaining mixture, preparing the sheets as instructed in step 1.

Chef's tips If you are baking more than one sheet of cookies in a non-convection oven, swap them around halfway through to make sure they cook evenly.

Use a good-quality jam as it will hold well and give a better flavor and color. You could also use different colored jams, such as apricot or marmalade.

Biscotti

The name of these spicy little cookies literally means "twice baked."
They are ideal served with ice cream, sorbet, warm fruit compote or even with a cup of coffee,
although they were traditionally served to be dipped into a glass of sweet wine.

Preparation time **25 minutes**
Total cooking time **1 hour 10 minutes**
Makes about 40

3 eggs
1 cup plus 2 tablespoons sugar
1 teaspoon salt
1 teaspoon vanilla extract
finely grated rind of 1 orange
finely grated rind of 1 lemon
3¹/2 cups all-purpose flour
2 teaspoons baking powder
¹/2 teaspoon ground cloves
³/4 cup blanched hazelnuts, lightly roasted and
coarsely chopped (see Chef's tips)
¹/3 cup blanched whole almonds, lightly roasted and
coarsely chopped (see Chef's tips)
¹/2 egg, lightly beaten
¹/3 cup sugar, for rolling
2 teaspoons ground cloves, for rolling

1 Preheat the oven to 325°F. Brush an 8-inch square pan with melted butter, line the base with waxed paper and coat the sides with a very thin layer of flour. Refrigerate until the butter has set. Bring water to a boil in the bottom of a double boiler and remove from the heat. Place the eggs, sugar, salt, vanilla and orange and lemon rind in the top of the double boiler and place it over the water, making sure the bottom of the insert does not touch the water. Beat with an electric mixer until the mixture is thick and mousse-like, and a trail is left when the beaters are lifted. Remove the bowl and continue to beat until the bowl feels cold and the mixture is cold, light and fluffy.

2 Sift together the flour, baking powder and ground cloves and, using a metal spoon or plastic spatula, fold it into the egg mixture. When the dry ingredients are almost mixed in, add the nuts and fold in until completely mixed. Press the dough into the pan and brush with the beaten egg. Bake for about 40 minutes, or until golden brown. Remove from the pan, peel off the waxed paper and allow to cool on a wire rack.

3 Reduce the oven temperature to 275°F. When the biscotti are cool, cut into three evenly sized pieces, approximately 8 x 2¹/2 inches. Cut each piece across the width into pieces approximately ⁵/8 inch wide. Place on a baking sheet, cut-side-down, and bake for another 30 minutes, or until the biscotti are golden brown and dry to the touch.

4 Mix the extra sugar with the ground cloves on a flat plate or a piece of waxed paper. Remove the biscotti from the baking sheet and roll in the flavored sugar.

Chef's tips To roast the hazelnuts and almonds, place on a baking sheet and roast in a 350°F oven for 3–5 minutes, taking care not to let the nuts burn.

For a variation, add ¹/2 cup chopped dried apricots and substitute ¹/2 teaspoon ground cinnamon for the ground cloves.

Honey wafers

These deliciously crispy and light cookies are ideal to use as an accompaniment for a scoop of vanilla ice cream or a fresh fruit sorbet.

Preparation time **10 minutes + 15 minutes refrigeration**
Total cooking time **3 minutes per baking sheet**
Makes about 30

2 tablespoons unsalted butter, at room temperature
1/4 cup confectioners' sugar
2 1/2 tablespoons honey
1/3 cup all-purpose flour
large pinch of salt
1 teaspoon ground cinnamon

1 Preheat the oven to 450°F. Brush two baking sheets with melted butter and refrigerate.

2 Using a wooden spoon or an electric mixer, cream the butter and sugar until light and fluffy. Beat in the honey until thoroughly mixed. Sift together the flour, salt and cinnamon and stir into the butter mixture. Cover the bowl with plastic wrap and refrigerate for about 15 minutes before using.

3 Cut a piece of thick cardboard or plastic to about 2 1/2 inches square. Cut a circle 2 inches in diameter from the center of the square to make a stencil. Prepare the cookies with the cardboard or plastic stencil, following the method in the Chef's techniques on page 62. Refrigerate the remaining mixture.

4 Bake for 2–3 minutes, or until golden brown. Using a palette knife or spatula, lift the wafers from the baking sheet while still hot. If the wafers set before you can remove them all from the baking sheet, return them to the oven to warm slightly. Cool on a wire rack. Repeat with the remaining mixture, preparing the sheets as instructed in step 1. Store in an airtight container.

Chef's tip These wafers become soft very quickly, so eat as soon as possible after baking.

Viennese fingers

These wonderful chocolate-dipped cookies simply melt in the mouth.

Preparation time **25 minutes**
Total cooking time **10 minutes per baking sheet**
Makes 16

❊

¹/₂ cup unsalted butter, at room temperature
2–3 drops vanilla extract
I teaspoon finely grated lemon rind
¹/₃ cup confectioners' sugar
I egg, lightly beaten
1¹/₄ cups all-purpose flour
6 oz. semisweet chocolate, chopped

1 Brush two baking sheets with melted butter and refrigerate. Preheat the oven to 400°F.
2 Using a wooden spoon or electric mixer, cream the butter, vanilla, lemon rind and sugar until light and fluffy. Gradually add the egg, a little at a time, beating well after each addition. Sift in the flour and stir to mix.
3 Spoon the mixture into a pastry bag with a ¹/₂-inch star nozzle. Pipe enough 2¹/₂–3-inch lengths to fill the prepared baking sheets, spacing them slightly apart. Bake for 7–10 minutes, or until golden brown. Cool on a wire rack. Repeat with the remaining mixture, preparing the cooled baking sheets as instructed in step 1.
4 Place the chocolate in the top of a double boiler over steaming water, off the stove. Make sure that the bottom of the insert doesn't touch the water. Stir until the chocolate melts. Dip one end of each cookie in the chocolate and cool on a tray covered with waxed paper.

Chef's tip For a variation, pipe the dough into rosettes about 1¹/₂ inches wide (see Chef's techniques, page 63). When cooked, divide the cookies into pairs. Spread the bottom of one with some jam, then stick the two together. Dust with confectioners' sugar and place in paper petits fours cases.

Brandy snaps with pistachio cream

These crisp, lacy, rolled wafer cookies are often served in England filled with brandy-flavored whipped cream. Here, they are filled with pistachio cream, but they are also delicious served plain or dipped in chocolate.

Preparation time **25 minutes + 30 minutes refrigeration**
Total cooking time **15 minutes per baking sheet**
Makes 32

❀

¹/4 cup unsalted butter
¹/4 cup light brown or Demerara sugar
2 tablespoons dark corn syrup
¹/2 cup all-purpose flour
small pinch of ground ginger
¹/3 cup shelled pistachios
²/3 cup whipping cream

1 Brush two baking sheets with melted butter.
2 Place the butter, sugar and corn syrup in a small saucepan. Stir gently over low heat until the sugar has dissolved. Cool for 1 minute. Sift the flour with the ginger and stir into the mixture, mixing well.
3 Transfer the mixture to a bowl and refrigerate for 30 minutes, or until cooled and firm. Preheat the oven to 350°F. Drop enough teaspoons of the mixture in small rounds to fill the baking sheets, spacing them at least 4 inches apart. Press down with the spoon to flatten slightly, and bake for 5–6 minutes, or until golden brown (see Chef's techniques, page 62).

4 Immediately loosen the brandy snaps from the baking sheet using a spatula and, working quickly, shape them around the handle of a wooden spoon (see Chef's techniques, page 62). If they begin to set before you have finished shaping, return them to the oven briefly to warm. Repeat with the remaining mixture, preparing the baking sheets as instructed in step 1. Warm the mixture a little if it has cooled too much to spoon easily.
5 Bring a small saucepan of water to a boil. Add the pistachios and simmer for 5 minutes, then drain. Transfer to a bowl of cold water and pop them out of their skins by pressing them between your finger and thumb. Chop coarsely and brown them under a preheated broiler for 1–2 minutes. Cool, then pound a third of the nuts into a paste in a pestle and mortar, or process in a blender or food processor. Lightly whip the cream, fold in the nut paste, then spoon into a pastry bag fitted with a small star or plain nozzle and carefully pipe into both ends of the brandy snaps. Decorate the ends with the remaining chopped pistachios.

Chef's tips The unfilled brandy snaps can be stored in an airtight container in a cool, dry place for a few days.
    Make very small brandy snaps to serve as petits fours with coffee at the end of a meal.

Quick oatmeal cookies

*A chewy and buttery cookie, with a hint of orange and vanilla,
to which you can add nuts, chocolate chips and sunflower seeds.*

Preparation time **15 minutes**
Total cooking time **12 minutes per baking sheet**
Makes about 36

I cup all-purpose flour
1/2 teaspoon baking soda
1/2 teaspoon baking powder
1/2 teaspoon salt
1/2 cup lightly packed soft brown sugar
1/2 cup sugar
1/2 cup unsalted butter
I egg, lightly beaten
I teaspoon vanilla extract
I tablespoon milk
I teaspoon finely grated orange rind
1 2/3 cups rolled oats
I cup raisins

1 Preheat the oven to 350°F. Line two baking sheets with waxed paper. Sift together the flour, baking soda, baking powder and salt.

2 Cream together the sugars and butter. Add the egg, vanilla and milk, and beat until smooth. Stir in the sifted ingredients and mix well. Stir in the grated orange rind, then the oats and raisins.

3 Scoop up balls of the dough with a tablespoon and drop enough of them to fill the prepared baking sheets, spacing them approximately 2 inches apart (see Chef's techniques, page 63). Bake for 10–12 minutes, or until just brown. Remove immediately from the baking sheets and cool on a wire rack. Repeat with the remaining mixture, preparing the sheets as in step 1.

Chef's tip If you are baking more than one sheet of cookies in a non-convection oven, swap them around halfway through, to make sure they cook evenly.

Fours poches

In French a poche may refer to a pastry bag, hence the name of these petits fours cookies that are piped onto baking sheets before being topped with either a cherry, almond or hazelnut.

*Preparation time **10 minutes + 30 minutes resting***
*Total cooking time **15 minutes***
*Makes **16–18***

☼ ☼

3/4 cup ground almonds
1/3 cup sugar
2 small egg whites
2 teaspoons apricot jam, strained
2 drops vanilla extract
2 drops almond extract
almond halves, for decoration
glacé (candied) cherry halves, for decoration
whole hazelnuts, for decoration

1 Preheat the oven to 350°F. Line two baking sheets with waxed paper. Sift the ground almonds and sugar twice and place in a bowl with one of the egg whites, the apricot jam, vanilla and almond extract. Stir together and add just enough of the remaining egg white to give a firm consistency—the mixture should be almost too thick to pipe.

2 Spoon the mixture into a pastry bag fitted with a 1/2-inch star nozzle and pipe 11/2-inch rosettes onto the paper (see Chef's techniques, page 63). Decorate the top of each rosette with either a half almond, half glacé cherry or whole hazelnut. Leave to stand at room temperature for 30 minutes.

3 Bake the cookies for 15 minutes, or until golden brown, but not too dark. Transfer to a wire rack to cool.

Chef's tips These cookies will keep in an airtight container for up to 2 weeks.

If you are baking more than one sheet of cookies in a non-convection oven, swap them around halfway through, to make sure they cook evenly.

Snickerdoodles

These citrus-flavored cookies with their cinnamon sugar coating have appeared under many different names in regional American cookbooks since the last century. In many Midwest cookbooks they are referred to as Snickerdoodles, as in this recipe.

*Preparation time **15 minutes + 30 minutes chilling***
*Total cooking time **12 minutes per baking sheet***
*Makes about **30***

2 cups all-purpose flour
1/2 teaspoon baking soda
1/4 teaspoon salt
large pinch of grated nutmeg
1/2 cup unsalted butter, at room temperature
3/4 cup sugar
I egg
I egg yolk
I teaspoon vanilla extract
I teaspoon finely grated lemon or orange rind
2 teaspoons ground cinnamon, to coat
2 tablespoons sugar, to coat

1 Preheat the oven to 375°F. Prepare two baking sheets by brushing with melted butter.

2 Sift together the flour, baking soda, salt and grated nutmeg. Cream together the butter and sugar and add the egg, egg yolk, vanilla and lemon or orange rind. Beat until light and fluffy. Add the sifted ingredients and mix well. Scrape down the sides, cover the bowl with a piece of plastic wrap and refrigerate for 30 minutes. Mix the cinnamon and sugar together in a small bowl.

3 Using a teaspoon, scoop up small amounts of the dough and roll them into balls about 1 inch in diameter. Roll the balls in the cinnamon sugar and use enough to fill the prepared baking sheets, spacing about 2 inches apart. Slightly flatten the balls and bake for about 12 minutes, or until the cookies are just starting to brown around the edges and slide easily from the baking sheet. Cool on a wire rack. Repeat with the remaining mixture, preparing the sheets as in step 1.

Chef's tip If you are baking more than one sheet of cookies in a non-convection oven, swap them around halfway through, to make sure they cook evenly.

Gingersnaps

The tantalizing spicy aroma of these cookies as they come out of the oven is bound to test your willpower. It will be difficult to wait for them to cool and become hard and crunchy as they should be.

*Preparation time **15 minutes + 1 hour 30 minutes***
  refrigeration
*Total cooking time **15 minutes per baking sheet***
Makes about 40

¹/4 cup unsalted butter, at room temperature
³/4 cup sugar
1 egg
¹/4 cup molasses
2 teaspoons white wine vinegar
2 cups bread or all-purpose flour
1¹/2 teaspoons baking soda
¹/2 teaspoon ground ginger
pinch of ground cinnamon
pinch of ground cloves
pinch of ground cardamom
sugar, to coat

1 Preheat the oven to 375°F. Line two baking sheets with waxed paper.

2 Using a wooden spoon or an electric mixer, cream together the butter and sugar until light and fluffy. Add the egg, a little at a time, beating well after each addition. Add the molasses and vinegar and mix well.

3 Sift together the flour, baking soda, ground ginger, cinnamon, cloves and cardamom and stir into the butter mixture. Bring a ball of dough together with your hands, wrap it in plastic wrap and refrigerate for about 1¹/2 hours, or until firm.

4 Divide the dough into four and, using the palms of your hands, roll each piece into a rope. Cut each rope into 10 pieces and roll the pieces into balls. Spread the sugar on a flat plate. Roll each ball through the sugar, place on the prepared sheets spaced well apart and press down slightly to flatten. Refrigerate the remaining dough until needed. Bake for about 10–15 minutes, or until golden brown. Repeat with the remaining mixture, preparing the sheets as instructed in step 1.

Chef's tips This cookie dough can be prepared in advance, rolled in the sugar and slightly flattened. Wrap in plastic wrap and freeze as individual pieces. To bake, place the frozen balls on a lined baking sheet and bake at 375°F for 20 minutes.

If you are baking more than one sheet of cookies in a non-convection oven, swap them around halfway through, to make sure they cook evenly.

Paintbox cookies

*Buy a variety of different sized paintbrushes and
the cookies become your canvas.*

Preparation time **25 minutes + 1 hour refrigeration**
Total cooking time **12 minutes per baking sheet**
Makes about 36

❀ ❀

1¼ cups unsalted butter, at room temperature
1½ cups sugar
2 eggs
2 teaspoons vanilla extract
3 cups all-purpose flour
½ teaspoon baking soda
1 teaspoon salt
4 egg yolks
red, blue, green and yellow food coloring

1 Preheat the oven to 350°F. Brush two baking sheets
with melted butter.
2 Cream the butter and sugar until light and fluffy.
Add the eggs and vanilla and beat well. Sift the flour,
baking soda and salt into the mixture and combine.
Wrap the dough in plastic wrap and refrigerate for about
1 hour, or until firm. If it becomes too hard, leave at
room temperature for about 20 minutes.
3 Place each egg yolk in a separate bowl. Add a
teaspoon of water and beat well with a fork. Add a few
drops of a different food color to each one.
4 Divide the dough in half; keep half refrigerated and
roll out the other half between two sheets of waxed
paper to about a 1/8–1/4-inch thickness (see Chef's
techniques, pages 63). Cut out shapes and use enough
to fill the prepared baking sheets. Use small
paintbrushes to paint the cookies, adding a little extra
water to the food colorings to create a more translucent
effect. Allow the "paint" to dry before baking.
5 Bake for 10–12 minutes, or until lightly colored.
Cool on a wire rack. Repeat with the remaining mixture,
preparing the baking sheets as instructed in step 1.

Peanut butter cookies

Peanut butter, whether smooth or chunky, is a favorite for many—children and adults alike. Is it any wonder then that these cookies are so popular?

*Preparation time **20 minutes + 1 hour refrigeration***
*Total cooking time **15 minutes per baking sheet***
Makes 30

¹/₂ cup unsalted butter, at room temperature
¹/₂ cup sugar
¹/₃ cup soft brown sugar
1 teaspoon vanilla extract
¹/₂ cup chunky peanut butter
1 egg, lightly beaten
1¹/₂ cups bread or all-purpose flour
2 teaspoons baking powder
small pinch of salt
¹/₂ cup unsalted peanuts, chopped and roasted
*   (see Chef's tips)*
²/₃ cup unsalted peanuts, to garnish

1 Line two baking sheets with waxed paper. Using an electric mixer, cream together the butter and sugars until light and fluffy. Add the vanilla and peanut butter and mix well.

2 Gradually add the egg, a little at a time, beating well after each addition. Sift the flour, baking powder and salt together, add to the butter mixture and mix well. Stir in the chopped peanuts. Scrape the mixture out of the bowl onto a large piece of plastic wrap, cover and refrigerate for about 1 hour, or until firm.

3 Divide the dough into three pieces. On a floured surface, roll each third into a rope. Cut each rope into 10 equal-sized pieces. Preheat the oven to 350°F.

4 Roll each piece of dough in your hands to make a smooth ball, then use enough balls of dough to fill the two prepared baking sheets, spacing the cookies well apart. Flatten slightly using a fork (if you find the dough sticks to the fork, dip the fork into a little flour). Arrange three peanuts on top of each cookie, then place in the oven to bake for about 12–15 minutes, or until golden brown. Transfer to a wire rack to cool. Repeat with the remaining dough, preparing the baking sheets as in step 1.

Chef's tips Once rolled into ropes, this dough can be stored in the freezer for up to 1 month.

To roast the peanuts, place on a baking sheet and roast in a 350°F oven for about 2–3 minutes, taking care not to let the nuts burn.

For a variation, add ¹/3 cup semisweet chocolate chips or replace the peanuts with hazelnuts.

Christmas cookies

*These little cookies with their jewel-like pieces of fruit are extremely popular.
Carefully arranged in decorative boxes, they make ideal Christmas presents.*

*Preparation time **25 minutes + 20 minutes refrigeration***
*Total cooking time **10 minutes***
Makes 12

2/3 cup unsalted butter, at room temperature
2/3 cup sugar
1 egg, beaten
finely grated rind of 1/2 lemon
finely grated rind of 1/2 orange
1/4 cup candied angelica or green glacé (candied)
  cherries, chopped
1/4 cup red glacé (candied) cherries, chopped
1/4 cup chopped mixed candied citrus peel
2 cups all-purpose flour
1/2 teaspoon ground mace
1/2 teaspoon ground cinnamon
1/2 teaspoon ground cloves
1/2 teaspoon ground nutmeg

1 Preheat the oven to 350°F. Brush two baking sheets with melted butter and refrigerate.
2 Using a wooden spoon or an electric mixer, cream together the butter and sugar. Gradually add the egg, beating well after each addition. Mix in the lemon and orange rind, angelica or green glacé cherries, red glacé cherries and mixed candied peel.
3 Sift the flour and ground spices into the mixture and combine. Using a plastic spatula, scrape onto a piece of plastic wrap and flatten lightly with your hand. Wrap in plastic wrap and refrigerate for 20 minutes until firm.
4 Place the dough between two sheets of waxed paper and roll out to an 1/8-inch thickness (see Chef's techniques, page 63). Cut out cookies using an assortment of 2-inch decorative cutters and place them on the prepared baking sheets, spacing slightly apart. Pierce each one with a fork several times and bake for 10 minutes, or until just golden brown and firm to the touch. Cool for 1 minute on the baking sheet, then using a palette knife, lift them onto a wire rack to cool.

Chef's tips Store these cookies in an airtight container. Placing a piece of white bread in the container will stop them from becoming stale.

For a variation, lightly beat 1 egg white and add enough sifted confectioners' sugar to make a very stiff paste. Spread a little frosting over each cookie and top with toasted sliced almonds or glacé cherries before baking. You could also change the spices from a mixture to just one spice, such as cinnamon.

Chef's techniques

◆

Making brandy snaps

Brandy snaps need to be shaped while hot. If they harden, put them back in the oven for 30 seconds.

Press a level teaspoon of the mixture down with a spoon to flatten slightly.

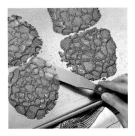

When the brandy snaps come out of the oven, loosen them from the baking sheet immediately using a spatula.

Working quickly while they are warm, shape them around the handle of a wooden spoon

Using a stencil

Using a plastic or thick cardboard stencil gives perfectly shaped cookies of an even thickness.

Place the stencil on a prepared baking sheet and spoon a little mixture into the hole.

Level off the mixture using a palette knife.

Remove the stencil carefully and repeat with enough of the mixture to fill the prepared baking sheets, spacing the cookies well apart.

When cooked, immediately remove the cookies from the sheet while they are still warm and pliable.

Making tuiles

Tuiles need to be shaped while still warm. Using a rolling pin gives the cookies their classic shape.

Drop a level teaspoon of the mixture onto a baking sheet and flatten slightly with a spoon.

Using a wet fork, evenly spread the mixture out so that it is very thin.

Remove the tuiles *from the* baking sheet while still hot and place on a rolling pin to shape. Transfer to a wire rack to cool.

Rolling and cutting dough

Rolling the dough gives an even thickness and coloring in baking and a professional finish.

Roll out the cookie dough between two sheets of waxed paper or plastic wrap.

Remove the waxed paper and cut out the cookies using shaped cutters. Place on the prepared baking sheet.

Piped cookies

Piping cookies gives them an even size and a neat appearance.

Pipe rosettes onto the prepared baking sheet, spacing them well apart. Alternatively, use a cookie press.

Drop cookies

The dough for drop cookies needs to be soft enough to fall from the spoon.

Scoop up balls of dough with a tablespoon and drop them onto the prepared baking sheet.

First published in the United States in 1998 by Periplus Editions (HK) Ltd., with editorial offices at
153 Milk Street, Boston, Massachusetts 02109.

Murdoch Books and Le Cordon Bleu thank the 32 masterchefs of all the Le Cordon Bleu Schools, whose knowledge and
expertise have made this book possible, especially: Chef Cliche (MOF), Chef Terrien, Chef Boucheret, Chef Duchêne (MOF),
Chef Guillut, Chef Steneck, Paris; Chef Males, Chef Walsh, Chef Hardy, London; Chef Chantefort, Chef Bertin, Chef Jambert,
Chef Honda, Tokyo; Chef Salembien, Chef Boutin, Chef Harris, Sydney; Chef Lawes, Adelaide; Chef Guiet, Chef Denis, Ottawa.
Of the many students who helped the Chefs test each recipe, a special mention to graduates David Welch and Allen Wertheim.
A very special acknowledgment to Directors Susan Eckstein, Great Britain, and Kathy Shaw, Paris, who have been responsible for
the coordination of the Le Cordon Bleu team throughout this series.

The Publisher and Le Cordon Bleu also wish to thank Carole Sweetnam for her help with this series.

First published in Australia in 1998 by Murdoch Books®

Managing Editor: Kay Halsey
Series Concept, Design and Art Direction: Juliet Cohen
Editor: Elizabeth Cotton
Food Director: Jody Vassallo
Food Editors: Lulu Grimes, Tracy Rutherford
US Editor: Linda Venturoni Wilson
Designer: Norman Baptista
Photographer: Luis Martin
Food Stylist: Rosemary Mellish
Food Preparation: Tracey Port
Chef's Techniques Photographer: Reg Morrison
Home Economists: Michelle Lawton, Kerrie Mullins, Tracey Port, Kerrie Ray

Library of Congress catalog card number: 98-85716
ISBN 962-593-443-X

Front cover: Melting moments

Distributed in the United States by
Charles E. Tuttle Co., Inc.
RR1 Box 231-5
North Clarendon, VT 05759
Tel: (802) 773-8930
Fax: (802) 773-6993

Printed in Singapore

05 04 03 02 01 00 99 98   10 9 8 7 6 5 4 3 2 1

Important: Some of the recipes in this book may include raw eggs, which can cause salmonella poisoning.
Those who might be at risk from this (the elderly, pregnant women, young children and those suffering
from immune deficiency diseases) should check with their physicians before eating raw eggs.